CHIPOTLE

Leda Scheintaub

Love Food ® is an imprint of Parragon Books Ltd

Parragon
Queen Street House
4 Queen Street
Bath BA1 1HE, UK

Copyright © Parragon Books Ltd 2008

Love Food ® and the accompanying heart device is a trademark of Parragon Books Ltd

ISBN: 978-1-4075-3401-5

Printed in China

Written by Leda Scheintaub
Designed by Andrew Easton at Ummagumma
Photography by Mike Cooper
Home economy by Lincoln Jefferson

Notes for the Reader

This book uses imperial, metric, and U.S. cup measurements. Follow the same units of measurement throughout; do not mix imperial and metric. All spoon measurements are level: teaspoons are assumed to be 5 ml, and tablespoons are assumed to be 15 ml. Unless otherwise stated, milk is assumed to be whole, eggs and individual vegetables, such as potatoes, are medium, and pepper is freshly ground black pepper.

The times given are an approximate guide only. Preparation times differ according to the techniques used by different people and the cooking times may also vary from those given as a result of the type of oven used. Optional ingredients, variations, or serving suggestions have not been included in the calculations.

Recipes using raw or very lightly cooked eggs should be avoided by infants, the elderly, pregnant women, convalescents, and anyone with a chronic condition. Pregnant and breastfeeding women are advised to avoid eating peanuts and peanut products. People with nut allergies should be aware that some of the prepared ingredients used in the recipes in this book may contain nuts. Always check the packaging before use.

contents

introduction

The chipotle, a smoked and dried jalapeño chile, is as integral a part of Mexican cooking today as it was in the days of the Aztecs. Lately you may have noticed that the chipotle is making its way into all kinds of establishments—from fast-food eateries to upscale restaurants. It is a favorite of many a celebrity chef, and has become downright trendy.

The first chapter of this book—Chipotle Essentials—introduces you to a variety of basic sauces, salsas, and condiments that are used in the recipes in the following chapters.

Although some of the recipes in this book are Mexican inspired, this is not a Mexican cookbook, and that's what makes it unique. The passion for chipotles extends beyond the traditional fare that Americans are used to—the goal of this book is to bring the chipotle into the American kitchen, updating American classics and touching on international cuisines including Indian and Asian.

HOW TO USE CHIPOTLE CHILES

Chipotles are available in three main forms: whole dried, powdered, or canned in adobo sauce. And adding a few drops of Chipotle Tabasco Sauce will enhance any dish. There are two varieties of chipotles—the dark red type, or chipotle morita, and the light brown type, or chipotle meco. They can be used interchangeably in the recipes in this book. All forms of chipotles can be found in Mexican groceries, some supermarkets, or any number of mail-order sources.

CHIPOTLE CHILI POWDER

Chipotle chili powder is simply ground dried chipotle chiles. It is the easiest form of chipotle to use—just measure and add to your dish. It tends to work well in soups, because it dissolves easily, and anywhere that you want to add a simple quick burst of smoky heat. You can make your own chili powder by toasting dried whole chiles, removing the seeds and stems, and blending in a blender.

CANNED CHIPOTLE CHILES IN ADOBO SAUCE

This is a commonly available form of chipotles, and quite inexpensive. Chipotles are packed in a vinegary sauce that contains tomatoes and sugar. They're easy to use and any leftovers can be frozen.

A NOTE ON HEAT LEVELS

The recipes in this book usually call for a range in the amount of chipotle, depending on how spicy you like your food. This is also because individual chiles can vary in heat, some being much hotter than others, and they will also vary in size.

Caution: Always wear plastic gloves while working with chiles to protect your hands from the heat. A plastic bag placed over the hand that handles the chile makes a simple makeshift glove. If you forget to cover your hands, make sure to wash them thoroughly afterward, and, above all, resist any temptation to rub your eyes.

Whole Dried Chiles

Whole dried chiles need to be toasted and soaked before using. Here's how to do it:

Preheat a small, heavy skillet (preferably cast iron) over medium heat. Place the chiles on the skillet, pressing down on them with a spatula for about 20 seconds to lightly toast, then turn over and toast on the other side for about 20 seconds. Remove the chiles from the skillet and place them in a bowl. Pour in hot water to cover and soak for about 30 minutes, or until fully hydrated, stirring occasionally or placing a plate on top of the chiles to keep them submerged. Drain the chiles and discard the soaking water. Remove the stems and seeds and proceed with your recipe. Keep in mind that some chiles will need to soak longer than others, depending on how fresh they are. Although it's best to use hot rather than boiling water to soak your chiles, particularly stubborn chiles may need a soak in boiling water to soften them. The recipes here call for discarding the soaking water, because it can have a bitter taste.

chapter 1
chipotle essentials

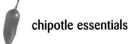

Fresh Tomato Salsa

Nothing pairs better with our favorite smoky chile than the tomato. Make this salsa often when tomatoes are in season. Serve it with Chilled Creamy Avocado Soup, Fish Tacos, or your scrambled eggs in the morning. Or just open up a bag of chips and dip in.

In a small bowl, combine the lime juice, chipotle powder, and salt to taste. Whisk together to dissolve the chipotle powder and salt.

In a large bowl, combine the tomatoes, onion, and garlic. Pour in the lime juice mixture and stir to fully coat. Stir in the cilantro. Taste and add more lime juice, chipotle powder, or salt if needed.

MAKES ABOUT 2 CUPS

2 tbsp fresh lime juice, or to taste

½ tsp chipotle powder, or to taste

1 lb/450 g (about 6 medium) plum tomatoes, cored, seeded, and finely chopped

1 small red onion, diced

1 garlic clove, minced

1 cup chopped fresh cilantro

salt

Green Salsa

Tomatillos are similar to green tomatoes but smaller and with a papery husk that is peeled off before using. They have a punchy, tangy flavor that contrasts perfectly with the smokiness of the chipotle. Use this salsa in the Tomatillo Guacamole, with Fish Tacos, or include it with roasted chicken or other meat or fish dishes.

Preheat the broiler, then preheat a small, heavy skillet (preferably cast iron) over medium heat. Place the chiles on the skillet, pressing down on them with a spatula for about 20 seconds to lightly toast them, then turn them over and toast on the other side for about 20 seconds. Remove the chiles from the skillet and place them in a bowl. Pour in hot water to cover and soak for about 30 minutes, or until fully hydrated, stirring occasionally or placing a plate on top of the chiles to keep them submerged.

While the chiles are soaking, place the tomatillos on a baking sheet and place under the broiler. Broil for about 5 minutes, or until softened with some black spots, then turn and broil on the other side for about 5 minutes. Remove from the oven and pour into the food processor or blender and set aside to cool.

Remove the chiles from their soaking liquid and remove the stems and seeds. Discard the liquid and roughly chop the chiles. Add the chiles and garlic to the tomatillos in the food processor or blender and blend until fully combined and thick. Add the cilantro and blend to combine. Season with salt to taste and refrigerate until ready to use. The salsa will keep up to 5 days in the refrigerator.

MAKES ABOUT 1$^1/_2$ CUPS

2 dried chipotle chiles

1 lb/450 g tomatillos, husked and cleaned

2 garlic cloves, peeled and chopped

1 cup chopped fresh cilantro

salt

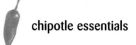

Everyday Chipotle Tomato Sauce

This recipe adds a bit of smoke and heat to your standard tomato sauce. Use it with Huevos Rancheros, Polenta Cakes, Beef Nacho Dip, in your favorite pasta or pizza recipe, or as a topping for tacos or enchiladas.

Preheat a small, heavy skillet (preferably cast iron) over medium heat. Place the chiles on the skillet, pressing down on them with a spatula for about 20 seconds to lightly toast, then turn over and toast on the other side for about 20 seconds. Remove the chiles from the skillet and place them in a bowl. Pour in hot water to cover and soak for about 30 minutes, or until fully hydrated, stirring occasionally or placing a plate on top of the chiles to keep them submerged. Drain the chiles and discard the soaking water. Remove the stems and seeds and finely mince the chiles.

In a medium saucepan, heat the oil over medium heat. Add the onion and sauté until softened, about 5 minutes. Add the chile and cook, stirring, for 2 minutes. Add the garlic and sauté until softened, about 1 minute. Crush the tomatoes with your hands directly into the pan, along with their juice. Add the vinegar, sugar, and salt to taste and bring to a simmer. Reduce the heat, partially cover the pan, and simmer for 30 minutes, stirring occasionally. Taste and add more salt, vinegar, or sugar if needed.

MAKES ABOUT 2 CUPS

1–2 dried chipotle chiles

2 tbsp extra virgin olive oil

1 medium yellow onion, chopped

2 garlic cloves, finely chopped

1 lb 12 oz/800 g canned whole
 tomatoes in juice

1 tsp cider vinegar, or to taste

1 tsp sugar, or to taste

salt

Smoky Citrus Dressing

Use this light and tangy dressing in the Pinto Bean and Corn Salad or in place of your standard vinaigrette on any green salad.

Combine all the ingredients with salt to taste in a lidded jar and shake to blend the dressing. Use immediately or store in the refrigerator for up to 3 days.

MAKES ³/₄ CUP

6 tbsp fresh lime juice

2 tbsp fresh lemon juice

1 garlic clove, minced

1 tsp chipotle powder, or to taste

1 tbsp maple syrup

¼ cup extra virgin olive oil

2 tsp cumin seeds, toasted (optional)

salt

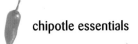

Smoky Chili Powder

This chili powder is used often in this book—in Spicy Mango on a Stick, Chili-Roasted Chickpeas and Pumpkin Seeds, and Chili-Flavored Pork Ribs, to name a few—so make some in advance to have plenty on hand.

Preheat a medium skillet (preferably cast iron) over medium heat. Place the cumin seeds in the skillet and toast, stirring, until lightly browned and aromatic, about 2 minutes. Transfer to the jar of a blender. Place the chiles on the skillet two at a time and toast, pressing down on them with the back of a metal spatula, until lightly browned and wisps of smoke escape when you press, 10 to 20 seconds on each side. (The smoother guajillo chiles will toast more quickly.)

Transfer the chiles to a plate to cool, then remove the stems and seeds and break them into a few pieces. Place in the blender, along with the oregano and garlic, and blend until broken down into a fine powder, shaking the jar a couple of times so the mixture can blend evenly. Let the powder settle for a couple of minutes before opening the jar to make sure your eyes avoid contact with the chili powder dust.

Transfer to an airtight jar until ready to use. The chili powder will keep for 6 months.

MAKES ABOUT $^1/_2$ CUP

2 tbsp cumin seeds

4 dried ancho chiles

2 dried guajillo chiles

2 dried chipotle chiles

2 tbsp dried oregano

2 tbsp garlic powder

Quick & Easy Smoky Chili Powder

If you don't have time to toast and grind your spices, try this version—combining your ingredients is all that's needed.

Thoroughly combine all the ingredients in a medium bowl. Transfer to an airtight container until ready to use.

MAKES $^1/_2$ CUP

2 tbsp ground cumin

1 tbsp chipotle chili powder

1 tbsp ancho chili powder

2 tbsp dried oregano, crumbled

2 tbsp garlic powder

17

Chipotle Paste

Chipotle Paste is the perfect base for any number of stews, soups, and marinades, and you'll see it used in this book in Tempeh in Coconut-Lemongrass Sauce, Hot, Sweet & Sour Shrimp, and South Indian Chicken Curry. It can be adapted to fit your tastes, so try a little experimenting—for example, add some minced lemongrass and ginger to make an Asian-style Chipotle Paste.

With the motor of a food processor running, drop the garlic cloves in through the hole in the top to mince. Add all the other ingredients and process until blended. Transfer to a container, cover, and refrigerate. The paste will keep for up to 2 weeks in the refrigerator and frozen for several months.

MAKES ABOUT 1 CUP

4 garlic cloves

7 oz/200 g canned chipotle chiles
  in adobo sauce

½ small white onion, minced

1 tsp dried oregano

1 tsp ground cumin

Chipotle Mayonnaise

Spice up your egg salad with this smoky mayonnaise, or use anytime in place of standard mayonnaise.

In a medium bowl, combine all the ingredients and whisk together to fully incorporate.

MAKES 1 CUP

1 cup prepared mayonnaise

¾ tsp chipotle powder, or to taste

1 tsp fresh lemon juice, or to taste

Chipotle Sour Cream

This is the perfect topping for baked potatoes, or in any savory recipe that calls for sour cream. Try it with Huevos Rancheros, Beef Nacho Dip, Black Bean Chili, or Fish Tacos.

In a medium bowl, combine the sour cream and chipotles. Whisk together to fully incorporate.

MAKES 1 CUP

1 cup sour cream

1 tbsp minced canned chipotles in adobo sauce or ¾ tsp chipotle powder, or to taste

Chipotle Butter

Use this butter on hot biscuits, to top off steak, or in place of plain butter whenever you want to add a little heat.

Place all the ingredients in a food processor and blend until fully incorporated. Place the mixture in a container, cover, and refrigerate until ready to use.

MAKES $1/_2$ CUP

½ cup (1 stick) unsalted butter, softened

4 tsp minced canned chipotle chiles in adobo sauce, or to taste

1 tbsp adobo sauce from canned chipotle chiles

1½ tsp fresh lime zest

2 tsp fresh lime juice

¼ tsp salt

Chipotle Ketchup

For an instant version, just combine the ketchup with the chipotle powder—no cooking required.

Combine all the ingredients with salt to taste in a small saucepan and place over medium heat. Bring to a simmer and cook, stirring frequently, for 5 minutes, or until the ketchup is slightly thickened. Remove from the heat and cool. Transfer to a jar, cover, and refrigerate until ready to use.

MAKES 1 CUP

1 cup prepared ketchup

½ tsp Worcestershire sauce

½ tsp light brown sugar

1 tbsp fresh lemon juice, or to taste

1½ tsp chipotle powder, or to taste

1 tsp ground cumin

½ tsp ground turmeric

¼ tsp ground ginger

salt

Chipotle Mustard

The simple addition of chipotle powder completely transforms this standard condiment.

Place the ingredients in a small bowl and stir to thoroughly combine. Transfer to a jar, cover, and refrigerate until ready to use.

MAKES ¹/₂ CUP

½ cup Dijon-style mustard

1 tsp chipotle powder, or to taste

Quick Pickled Onions

These sweet, spicy, and tangy onions require no heating, so they're easy to make anytime. Include them at the table with all your standard condiments—salsa, sour cream, and the like, to serve with tacos, enchiladas, roasted meats, and breakfast dishes, or top off a Smoky Hamburger with a couple of rings.

In a medium bowl, combine the vinegar, sugar, chipotle powder, and salt to taste. Whisk to dissolve the sugar. Place the onions in a heavy-duty, zip-top bag and pour the marinade over the onions. Toss to coat. Cover and refrigerate for 30 minutes, moving the mixture around a couple of times to evenly distribute the marinade. Drain before serving.

MAKES ABOUT 2 CUPS

1 cup distilled white vinegar

½ cup sugar

1 tsp chipotle powder, or to taste

2 medium red onions, cut into rings

salt

chapter 2
breakfast

Huevos Rancheros

This is the quintessential Mexican breakfast dish—corn tortillas topped with fried eggs and drenched with a spicy tomato sauce. Finishing with Chipotle Tabasco Sauce and Chipotle Sour Cream will satisfy even the most serious chipotle aficionado.

Heat the tortillas by placing them directly over a medium gas flame or in a preheated skillet over medium heat. Heat for about 20 seconds, until hot, turning often and watching that they don't burn. Wrap in a dish towel to keep warm while you make the eggs.

In a large nonstick skillet, heat 1 tablespoon of the butter over medium heat. Break 4 of the eggs into the skillet, being careful to avoid breaking the yolks, and cook to desired doneness, 3–5 minutes, covering the pan for the last minute or so to evenly cook through. Remove from the skillet and keep warm while you cook the second batch, coating the pan with the remaining 1 tablespoon butter before adding the eggs. Season with salt.

Spoon some of the sauce onto plates and top with 2 slightly overlapping tortillas. Place an egg on top of each tortilla, and top with the remaining sauce. Garnish with queso fresco, chopped onion, and cilantro. Serve with Chipotle Tabasco Sauce and chipotle sour cream if you like.

SERVES 4

8 corn tortillas

2 tbsp unsalted butter

8 large eggs

salt

to serve

Everyday Chipotle Tomato Sauce
   (see page 13)

crumbled queso fresco (Mexican fresh
   white cheese) or feta cheese

chopped white onion

chopped fresh cilantro

Chipotle Tabasco Sauce (optional)

Chipotle Sour Cream (see page 21) or
   regular sour cream (optional)

Scrambled Eggs with Tomatillo Guacamole

This guacamole pairs perfectly with scrambled eggs, but it can be served any time of day with any meal, or simply with chips for dipping. You can easily scale the recipe down, using about $1/2$ cup salsa for each avocado. The Green Salsa will make the guacamole tangy and spicy, but you may want to add a little lime juice or chipotle powder as needed.

To make the tomatillo guacamole, cut the avocados in half and scoop out the flesh. Place in a large bowl and coarsely mash with a fork, potato masher, or whisk. Fold in the salsa and season with salt and lime juice to taste, and add chipotle powder if you'd like a little more heat. Cover with plastic wrap and refrigerate until ready to serve—ideally about a half hour after making.

To make the scrambled eggs, crack the eggs into a large bowl, add the milk, and whisk until frothy. Season with salt to taste. In a large nonstick skillet, melt the butter over medium heat. Add the eggs and cook to desired firmness, stirring constantly with a heatproof spatula.

Spoon the scrambled eggs onto plates along with the guacamole. Serve with tortillas, tomato salsa, cheese, and Chipotle Tabasco Sauce.

SERVES 4

tomatillo guacamole
3 large ripe avocados
Green Salsa (see page 10)
fresh lime juice
chipotle powder
salt

scrambled eggs
8 large eggs
2 tbsp milk
1 tbsp butter
salt

to serve
corn tortillas
Fresh Tomato Salsa (see page 9)
grated cheddar cheese
Chipotle Tabasco Sauce

Mochi Waffles with Chipotle Crème Fraîche

This is an exotic breakfast recipe to surprise your guests with. Mochi is made from sweet rice that is pounded until sticky and formed into squares—a popular treat in Japan and other Asian countries that you can find in natural food stores. It puffs up when cooked, so it makes for a perfect waffle base—no measuring, mixing, or pouring required!

In a medium bowl, whisk together the crème fraîche, cherries, and chipotle powder. Set aside.

Preheat the waffle iron. Cut the mochi into 4 equal-size squares. One or two at a time, place the squares in the waffle iron and heat for 3–5 minutes, until puffed and crisp. You may need to hold the waffle iron down for the first few seconds until the mochi has softened enough for the iron to close easily.

Place the mochi squares on serving plates. Drizzle with butter and maple syrup and top with a dollop of the crème fraîche mixture.

SERVES 4

½ cup crème fraîche

1 tbsp finely chopped dried tart cherries

pinch of chipotle powder

12½ oz/365 g package whole grain mochi

melted butter, to serve

warmed maple syrup, to serve

Cheddar Biscuits with Sun-Dried Tomatoes & Chipotle Butter

Nothing beats biscuits straight from the oven, so time it that they're ready just as you sit down to eat, and serve with generous amounts of Chipotle Butter.

Preheat the oven to 400°F/200°C. Grease a baking sheet and set aside.

Soak the sun-dried tomatoes in a small bowl with hot water to cover for 10 minutes. Drain, squeeze out excess liquid, and mince. Set aside.

In a large bowl, sift together the flour, baking powder, baking soda, and salt. Stir in the chipotle powder, mustard, and basil. Cut in the butter using a pastry blender or rub it in with your fingertips until completely incorporated. Fold in the cheese and sun-dried tomatoes.

Using a kitchen fork, stir in the buttermilk. The dough will be slightly sticky. Gather the dough into a ball with your hands and turn out onto a well-floured work surface. With floured hands, pat the dough $^1/_2$ inch/1 cm thick and cut into 12 squares using a floured knife or dough scraper.

Place the squares on the baking sheet with a little space between them and bake for about 15 minutes, or until well risen and very lightly browned. Remove from the oven and serve immediately with chipotle butter.

MAKES 12 BISCUITS

6 tbsp unsalted butter, chilled, plus extra for greasing

4 sun-dried tomatoes (not packed in oil)

2½ cups all-purpose flour

1 tbsp baking powder

½ tsp baking soda

½ tsp salt

½ tsp chipotle powder

½ tsp dry mustard

1 tsp dried basil

1 cup coarsely grated sharp cheddar cheese

¾ cup buttermilk

Chipotle Butter (see page 22), to serve

Polenta Cakes with Chipotle Tomato Sauce

Polenta cakes make a great addition to the breakfast table—a nice alternative to your standard potatoes or grits. Or skip the firming and baking steps and serve in bowls as you would regular polenta.

Preheat a small, heavy skillet (preferably cast iron) over medium heat. Place the chiles on the skillet, pressing down on them with a spatula for about 20 seconds to lightly toast, then turn over and toast on the other side for about 20 seconds. Remove the chiles from the skillet and place them in a bowl. Pour in hot water to cover and soak for about 30 minutes, or until fully hydrated, stirring occasionally or placing a plate on top of the chiles to keep them submerged. Drain the chiles, remove the stems and seeds, and finely mince.

In a large saucepan, bring the water to a boil over medium–high heat and add a little salt. Turn down the heat, add the cream and bring just to a simmer. Slowly whisk in the polenta and add the minced chiles. Reduce the heat to medium–low and simmer, whisking constantly, until the mixture is very thick but still pourable, about 20 minutes.

Remove from the heat and whisk in the butter, 2 tablespoons of the Parmesan cheese, and the mascarpone cheese, if using. Season with salt to taste.

Pour the polenta into a small baking pan and spread evenly with a heatproof spatula. Set aside for about 1 hour to firm up, or cover and refrigerate overnight.

Preheat the oven to 375°F/190°C. Line another, slightly larger, baking pan. Cut the polenta into squares and transfer to the oiled baking pan. Spread the sauce over the top and top with the cheddar cheese and remaining 2 tablespoons of Parmesan cheese. Bake for about 20 minutes, until the cheese is bubbly.

SERVES 4

1–2 dried chipotle chiles

2 cups water

½ cup heavy cream

½ cup coarse polenta

1 tbsp unsalted butter

¼ cup grated Parmesan cheese

2 tbsp mascarpone cheese (optional)

salt

1 cup Everyday Chipotle Tomato Sauce (see page 13)

½ cup coarsely grated cheddar cheese

Grown-Up Hot Chocolate

Adding a hint of chipotle to hot chocolate gives it a decidedly richer, more complex flavor that adults will savor. For an after-dinner treat, spike with a splash of Grand Marnier or your favorite coffee liqueur.

In a small saucepan, combine the milk and chocolate. Place over medium–low heat and cook, whisking constantly, until the chocolate melts and the mixture comes to a simmer. Whisk in the chipotle powder and orange zest.

Pour into cups, dust with nutmeg, and serve.

SERVES 4

2 cups milk

4 oz/115 g bittersweet or semisweet
   chocolate, cut into pieces

large pinch of chipotle powder,
   or to taste

½ tsp grated orange zest

freshly grated nutmeg, for dusting

chapter 3
snacks & appetizers

Spicy Mango on a Stick

This is Mexican street food at its best—sweet, tangy, salty, and smoky-hot all rolled into one. And what could be more fun than eating a mango on a stick? Traditionally the mango is cut to resemble a flower, and you bite off the petals.

Using a paring knife, carefully make an incision in the bottom of the mango extending about 1 inch/2.5 cm in. Insert an ice pop stick into the hole (if you don't have one handy, a chopstick makes a good stand-in).

Peel the mango using a sturdy vegetable peeler. Then score the mango to create petal shapes, as shown on page 44 (or make your own design—be creative).

Squeeze the lime over the mango, then sprinkle with chili powder and Chipotle Tabasco Sauce if you'd like a little more heat. Sprinkle with salt.

SERVES 1

1 mango

½ lime

Smoky Chili Powder (see page 17), to taste

Chipotle Tabasco Sauce, to taste (optional)

salt

Chili-Roasted Chickpeas

These two snacks are healthy and delicious alternatives to chips and make great party food. You may want to scale up the quantities, because they'll go fast.

Preheat the oven to 425°F/220°C and grease a large baking sheet. Pat the chickpeas dry with paper towels to remove excess moisture.

In a large bowl, combine the chickpeas with the oil and salt to taste. Place on the baking sheet in one layer and roast, shaking the pan occasionally, for about 20 minutes, until the chickpeas are golden brown. Return the chickpeas to the bowl and toss with the chili powder. Taste and add more salt or chili powder if needed. Serve hot or at room temperature.

MAKES 3 CUPS

30 oz/850 g canned chickpeas, drained and rinsed, or 3 cups cooked dried chickpeas

3 tbsp extra virgin olive oil, plus extra for greasing

1 tsp Smoky Chili Powder (see page 17), or to taste

salt

Chili-Roasted Pumpkin Seeds

These are so easy to make and thoroughly addictive—they'll quickly become a favorite snack.

Preheat a medium skillet (preferably cast iron) over medium heat.

In a medium bowl, toss together the pumpkin seeds, oil, chili powder, and salt to taste. Add the pumpkin seeds to the skillet and cook, stirring constantly, for about 5 minutes, until lightly browned and fragrant. Remove from the heat and transfer to a bowl to cool.

MAKES 1 CUP

1 cup raw pumpkin seeds

1 tbsp extra virgin olive oil

1 tsp Smoky Chili Powder (see page 17)

salt

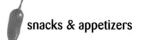

Spiked Jicama Salad

Jicama is a large root vegetable with thick tan skin and white flesh. It's wonderfully crisp so it is often used raw, as in this version of a traditional Mexican favorite.

In a medium bowl, combine the orange juice, lime juice, chili powder, and salt to taste. Whisk to dissolve the chili powder and salt.

Place the jicama in a large bowl, add the citrus juice mixture, and toss to coat. Taste and add more salt if needed. Add the mint and toss to coat.

SERVES 4–6

¼ cup fresh orange juice

¼ cup fresh lime juice

1½ tsp Smoky Chili Powder
   (see page 17), or to taste

1 medium jicama, peeled and cut into
   thin strips

½ cup chopped fresh mint

salt

Pinto Bean & Corn Salad with Cumin-Lime Dressing

If you're in a hurry, feel free to use prepared ingredients—jarred bell peppers, canned beans, and frozen and defrosted corn kernels—for an equally tasty salad.

Roast the bell peppers directly over a gas flame or place under the broiler, turning with tongs until all sides are blackened. Place the peppers in a heatproof bowl, cover with a large plate, and set aside for 20 minutes. Remove the peppers from the bowl. Remove the skin, stems, and seeds, and chop.

Combine the beans, corn kernels, onion, tomatoes, and bell peppers in a large bowl. Add enough dressing to coat, along with the Chipotle Tabasco Sauce. Taste and add more Chipotle Tabasco Sauce if you'd like a little more heat and season with salt if needed. Stir in the cilantro and top with the cheese if using. Serve cold or at room temperature.

SERVES 6

2 red bell peppers

30 oz/850 g canned cooked pinto beans, drained and rinsed

2 cups corn kernels (from 2–3 ears of corn)

1 small red onion, diced

2 plum tomatoes, cored, seeded, and chopped

4–6 tbsp Smoky Citrus Dressing (see page 14)

2 tsp Chipotle Tabasco Sauce, or to taste

1 cup chopped fresh cilantro

½ cup crumbled feta cheese (optional)

salt

Hummus with Roasted Garlic & Poblano Chiles

This might seem like a lot of garlic, but roasting mellows the garlic and lends a slightly sweet, buttery flavor to the hummus. Serve with tortilla chips, toasted pita chips, or carrot, celery, and jicama sticks.

Preheat the oven to 375°F/190°C. Peel off the papery outer layers of the garlic head and cut off the top ¹/₂ inch/1 cm. Place the garlic on a piece of aluminum foil large enough to fully wrap it. Drizzle with a little oil and sprinkle with salt. Wrap in the foil and roast for about 45 minutes, or until the garlic cloves are soft enough to slide out of the skin when pressed. Let cool, then pop the cloves out from the skin.

Roast the poblano chile directly over a gas flame or place under the broiler, turning with tongs until all sides are blackened. Place the chile in a heatproof bowl, cover with a large plate, and set aside for 20 minutes. Remove the chile from the bowl. Remove the skin, stems, and seeds, and finely chop.

In a food processor, combine the chickpeas, tahini, roasted garlic, chili powder, cumin, canned chipotles, oil, lime juice, and salt to taste and process until combined. With the motor running, add water, up to ¹/₂ cup, through the hole in the feed tube, until the mixture is smooth, scraping down the sides of the machine a couple of times. Fold in the poblano chiles. Taste and add more lime juice or salt if needed. Serve garnished with the whole chickpeas and a dusting of chili powder.

MAKES ABOUT 2 CUPS

1 head garlic

¹/₃ cup extra virgin olive oil, plus extra for roasting the garlic

1 large poblano chile

2 cups drained cooked or canned chickpeas, plus whole chickpeas for garnish

¹/₃ cup tahini (sesame paste)

1 tsp Smoky Chili Powder (see page 17), plus extra for garnish

1 tsp ground cumin

1–2 tsp chopped canned chipotle chiles in adobo sauce

3 tbsp fresh lime juice, or to taste

salt

Jalapeño Bhajis

Here the chipotle reconnects with its former self—the jalapeño—in this take on the bhaji, an Indian vegetable fritter. The amchoor powder provides a tangy flavor and gram flour holds the batter together without the use of eggs. Both can be found in Indian specialty markets.

Make a slit down the length of the jalapeños and halfway around the tops just under the stems. Carefully open up the jalapeños and remove the seeds and membranes using the back of a small spoon.

Place the sesame seeds in a spice grinder and grind to a fine paste. Transfer to a bowl, add the cumin, amchoor powder, chipotles, lime juice, water, and salt, and mix together.

To make the batter, whisk together the gram flour, rice flour, turmeric, baking soda, and salt in a medium bowl. Whisk in the water until smooth.

In a medium saucepan, heat 6 inches/15 cm of oil to 375°F/190°C.

Coat the inside of each jalapeño with about 1 teaspoon of the filling. Top with a very thin coating of the batter (this prevents the filling from leaking out), then dip the jalapeños in the batter, turning to evenly coat. Remove from the batter, letting any excess drip off.

Place the jalapeños in the oil, one or two at a time, and fry for about 5 minutes, until nicely browned and crisp. Remove with a slotted spoon to paper towels to drain and sprinkle with amchoor powder and salt. Serve immediately.

MAKES 12 BHAJIS

jalapeños and filling

12 large jalapeño chiles

2 tbsp sesame seeds

2 tsp ground cumin

2 tsp amchoor (dried mango) powder

2 tbsp minced canned chipotle chiles in adobo sauce

2 tsp fresh lime juice

2 tsp water

large pinch of salt

batter

2 cups gram (chickpea) flour

2 tbsp rice flour

½ tsp ground turmeric

¼ tsp baking soda

¼ tsp salt

1½ cups water

vegetable oil, for frying

amchoor powder and salt, for sprinkling

Shrimp & Squid Ceviche

Chipotles and citrus pair perfectly here and showcase the freshness of the seafood. If you don't have sake on hand, you can substitute white wine. For an elegant presentation, serve in martini glasses.

In a large bowl, whisk together the orange juice, lime juice, sake, Chipotle Tabasco Sauce, sugar, onion, orange zest, and salt to taste.

Bring a large saucepan of salted water to a simmer. Add the shrimp and cook until just cooked through, about 1 minute. Add the squid and cook until just tender, about 40 seconds.

Drain the shrimp and squid well and add to the marinade. Place in the refrigerator for 1 hour to marinate, stirring occasionally. Stir in the cilantro just before serving. Serve with lime wedges and tortilla chips for scooping.

SERVES 4

¼ cup fresh orange juice

½ cup fresh lime juice

1 tbsp sake

2 tbsp Chipotle Tabasco Sauce, or to taste

2 tsp sugar

1 medium red onion, diced

1 tsp grated orange zest

8 oz/225 g medium shrimp, peeled and deveined

8 oz/225 g squid, cleaned, tentacles separated and chopped, bodies cut into ¼ inch/5 mm rings

¼ cup chopped fresh cilantro, plus more to garnish

salt

lime wedges, to serve

tortilla chips, to serve

Beef Nacho Dip

This quick and easy nacho recipe requires no baking or assembling—simply prepare the beef and lay out the toppings for your guests to choose from.

In a large skillet, heat the oil over medium–high heat. Add the beef and sauté until browned, breaking it up with a wooden spoon, for about 5 minutes. Add the chili powder and stir until evenly distributed and aromatic. Add the corn kernels and tomato sauce.

Bring to a simmer, then reduce the heat, partially cover the skillet, and simmer, stirring occasionally, for about 10 minutes, until the beef is cooked through. Season with salt to taste. Stir in the cilantro and spoon into bowls. Have your toppings ready and pass them around. Serve with the tortilla chips for scooping.

SERVES 4–6

1 tbsp extra virgin olive oil

1 lb/450 g ground beef

1 tbsp Smoky Chili Powder
  (see page 17)

½ cup frozen corn kernels

Everyday Chipotle Tomato Sauce
  (see page 13)

½ cup chopped fresh cilantro

salt

tortilla chips, to serve

suggested toppings

grated cheddar cheese

Chipotle Sour Cream (see page 21)
  or regular sour cream

Chipotle Tabasco Sauce

shredded lettuce

chapter 4
soups

Smoky Gazpacho

You'll need to make this soup at least an hour in advance—or better yet, the day before—to fully allow the flavors to come out.

In a large bowl, combine the tomatoes, cucumber, onion, pepper, garlic, vinegar, lime juice, oil, cilantro, and salt to taste.

Place the tomato juice and chipotles in a blender and blend to puree the chipotles. Add half of the vegetable mixture and blend to a chunky puree.

Return the puree to the bowl and stir to combine with the chopped vegetables. Taste and adjust the seasonings, adding more lime juice or salt if needed.

Chill, covered, for at least 1 hour, until cold. Spoon into bowls and serve garnished with cilantro.

SERVES 4

1 lb/450 g tomatoes (about 2 large tomatoes), peeled, cored, seeded, and finely chopped

1 small cucumber, peeled, seeded, and finely chopped

½ medium red onion, finely chopped

1 small red bell pepper, cored and finely chopped

2 garlic cloves, minced

1 tbsp red wine vinegar

1 tbsp fresh lime juice, or to taste

1 tbsp extra virgin olive oil

½ cup loosely packed, chopped fresh cilantro, plus more to garnish

1½ cups unsalted tomato juice

2 tsp minced canned chipotle chiles in adobo sauce, or to taste

salt

Chilled Creamy Avocado Soup with Fresh Tomato Salsa

The smoky heat of the salsa contrasts perfectly with this light and refreshing summer soup. Season the soup lightly.

Using a kitchen spoon, scoop the flesh from the avocados and place in a blender. Add the lime juice and 1 cup of the water and blend until smooth. Add the remaining 1 cup of water, the yogurt, and salt to taste and blend until smooth. Taste and add additional salt or lime juice if needed.

Transfer to a container, cover, and refrigerate for at least 1 hour, until cold. Spoon into bowls and serve, topped with the salsa.

SERVES 4

3 large ripe avocados

2 tbsp fresh lime juice, or to taste

2 cups water

1 cup plain yogurt

salt

Fresh Tomato Salsa (see page 9), to serve

Roasted Butternut Squash Soup with Orange & Fennel

Celebrate the arrival of fall with this beautiful seasonal soup. Roasting intensifies the flavor of the squash and the orange juice enhances its sweetness.

Preheat the oven to 375°F/190°C and oil a baking pan. Preheat a small, heavy skillet (preferably cast iron) over medium heat. Place the chiles on the skillet, pressing down on them with a spatula for about 20 seconds to lightly toast, then turn over and toast on the other side for about 20 seconds. Remove the chiles from the skillet and place them in a bowl. Pour in hot water to cover and soak for about 30 minutes, or until fully hydrated, stirring occasionally or placing a plate on top of the chiles to keep them submerged. Drain the chiles and discard the soaking liquid. Remove the stems and seeds from the chiles and finely mince.

Place the squash in a large bowl, add the oil, and toss to coat. Sprinkle with salt and toss. Place the squash in the baking pan in one layer and bake for about 45 minutes, until browned and tender when pierced with a fork, turning the pieces occasionally. Return the squash to the bowl.

Warm the butter in a large saucepan over medium–low heat. Add the fennel, shallots, garlic, orange zest, and minced chipotles. Cover the pan and cook for 15 minutes, or until the vegetables are softened but not browned. Add the cumin and stir for 1 minute. Raise the heat, add the squash, orange juice, and water and bring to a simmer. Partially cover the pan and simmer for 15 minutes to combine the flavors. Add the cream and simmer for 5 minutes. Season with salt to taste.

Transfer the soup, in batches, to a blender and blend until smooth, adding water if needed to reach desired consistency. Return the soup to the pot and add the lemon juice and salt to taste if needed. Gently rewarm. Spoon into soup bowls, garnish with the fennel fronds, and serve.

SERVES 4–6

2 dried chipotle chiles

1 large butternut squash, peeled, cut in half, seeded, and cut into 1 inch/2.5 cm cubes

2 tbsp extra virgin olive oil, plus extra for brushing

2 tbsp unsalted butter

1 small fennel bulb, trimmed and chopped, fronds reserved for garnish

2 shallots, chopped

2 garlic cloves, chopped

1 tsp grated orange zest

2 tsp ground cumin

¾ cup orange juice

1 cup water

1 cup heavy cream

1 tbsp fresh lemon juice, or to taste

salt

Coconut Soup with Mussels

This rich and spicy soup is simple to make but elegant enough to serve for a special-occasion meal.

In a large saucepan, heat the butter over medium–high heat. Add the shallots and garlic and cook, stirring, for about 2 minutes, until softened. Add the mussels and wine, cover the pan, and cook, shaking the pan every couple of minutes, until the mussels have opened, about 5 minutes. Discard any unopened mussels.

Using a slotted spoon, scoop the mussels out of the pan and remove them from their shells. Place the pan back over medium–high heat and cook until the liquid is reduced by about half, about 5 minutes. Add the coconut milk, chipotle powder, curry powder, and salt to taste. Bring to a simmer, then reduce the heat to medium and simmer, uncovered, for 20 minutes to combine the flavors and thicken a little.

Return the mussels to the soup and heat to warm through. Add the lemon juice, taste, and add more salt or lemon juice if needed. Serve with lemon wedges and crusty bread.

SERVES 4

2 tbsp unsalted butter
2 shallots, finely chopped
1 garlic clove, finely chopped
2 lb/900 g mussels, cleaned
1 cup dry white wine
28 fl oz/800 ml canned coconut milk
1 tsp chipotle powder
1 tsp curry powder
2 tsp fresh lemon juice, or to taste
salt
lemon wedges, to serve
crusty bread, to serve

Chicken Dumpling Soup

This is pure winter comfort food with a bit of added heat. The soup gets a flavor boost by cooking the chicken in chicken stock. It's quite hearty—serve with a salad and you'll have a complete meal.

In a large saucepan, bring the chicken stock to a boil. Add the onion, carrot, celery, garlic, chipotle powder, and thyme and bring to a simmer.

Add the chicken, bring back to a simmer, then reduce the heat and simmer, uncovered, for about 45 minutes, until the chicken is tender and falling off the bone.

Meanwhile, make the dumplings. Sift the flour, baking powder, and salt into a medium bowl. Rub the butter into the dry ingredients until incorporated. Add the milk and thyme and stir with a fork to combine. Divide the dough into 16 walnut-size dumplings and roll them into a ball. Place on a large plate and set aside.

Remove the chicken from the pan and strain the stock, pressing on the solids to extract the liquid. Return the stock to the pan. Remove the chicken meat from the bone and shred it. Return the chicken to the pan and bring the soup to a simmer. Taste and season with salt if needed.

Lay the dumplings onto the surface of the soup, cover, and simmer for 10 minutes, or until cooked through and puffed. Spoon into bowls and serve garnished with the thyme leaves.

SERVES 4

soup

6 cups low-sodium chicken stock

1 small yellow onion, peeled and quartered

1 small carrot, roughly chopped

1 celery stalk, roughly chopped

2 garlic cloves, peeled

½–1 tsp chipotle powder, or to taste

½ bunch thyme

2 bone-in chicken thighs

salt

thyme leaves, for garnish

dumplings

1 cup all-purpose flour

1½ tsp baking powder

¼ tsp salt

2 tbsp unsalted butter, cut into ½ inch/1 cm pieces

½ cup milk

1 tbsp minced thyme leaves

Beef & Barley Soup

This take on beef and barley soup is influenced by the spices used in the classic Vietnamese pho soup—ginger, star anise, cinnamon, and cloves.

In a large saucepan, heat the oil over medium–high heat. Add the beef and cook for about 10 minutes, until browned on all sides. Using a slotted spoon, remove the beef from the pan and place in a bowl. Reduce the heat to medium, add the celery, onion, ginger, and barley, and sauté for about 10 minutes, until the onion is softened and golden. Add the star anise, cinnamon stick, cloves, and chipotle powder and cook for about 2 minutes, until aromatic.

Return the beef to the pan, add the beef stock, water, and fish sauce, and bring to a boil. Reduce the heat and simmer, uncovered, for about 1–1¹/₂ hours, until the beef is tender. Using a slotted spoon, remove the beef from the pan. Cool slightly, then shred the meat. Return the beef to the pan and cook to heat through. Add the lime juice. Taste and add additional fish sauce or lime juice if needed. Stir in the cilantro, mint, and scallions. Spoon into soup bowls and serve.

SERVES 4

2 tbsp peanut oil

1 lb/450 g stewing beef

2 celery stalks, chopped

1 medium onion, chopped

2 tsp finely chopped fresh ginger

¼ cup pearl barley

2 star anise

½ cinnamon stick

2 cloves

1 tsp chipotle powder, or to taste

4 cups/950 ml low-sodium beef stock

5 cups water

2 tbsp fish sauce, or to taste

1 tbsp fresh lime juice, or to taste

¼ cup chopped fresh cilantro

¼ cup chopped fresh mint

2 scallions, finely chopped

chapter 5
main courses

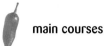

Black Bean Chili

This chili tastes even better the second day, so it's a perfect make-ahead dish. And it freezes well, so stock up your freezer to have plenty of chili on hand for the cold months of winter.

Place the beans in a large bowl and add water to cover by about 2 inches/5 cm. Let soak overnight.

In a large saucepan, heat the oil over medium heat. Add the onion and pepper and sauté for about 5 minutes, until softened. Add the garlic and cook for about 1 minute, until softened. Add the chili powder, cumin, paprika, cinnamon, and canned chipotles and cook, stirring, for 2 minutes, or until the seasonings are well mixed and aromatic.

Drain the beans and add them to the pan, along with the water. Bring to a simmer, then reduce the heat and simmer, partially covered, for 1–1¹/₂ hours, until the beans have softened and the mixture starts to thicken.

Crush the tomatoes with your hands directly into the pan, along with their juice. Add salt to taste and the vinegar and cook for 30 minutes, or until thickened. Taste and add additional salt or vinegar if needed. Stir in the cilantro. (If making ahead, don't add the cilantro until just before serving.) Serve, garnished with cilantro and with the cheese and sour cream alongside. Pass the Chipotle Tabasco Sauce around for those who like it hotter.

SERVES 4–6

2 cups dried black beans

3 tbsp extra virgin olive oil

1 medium yellow onion, chopped

1 red bell pepper, cored, seeded, and chopped

4 garlic cloves, chopped

1 tbsp Smoky Chili Powder (see page 17)

1 tbsp ground cumin

1 tsp paprika

½ tsp ground cinnamon

2 tbsp minced canned chipotle chiles in adobo sauce, or to taste

5 cups water

1 lb 12 oz/800 g canned whole tomatoes in juice

1 tbsp cider vinegar, or to taste

1 cup chopped fresh cilantro, plus extra for garnish

salt

to serve

grated cheddar cheese

Chipotle Sour Cream (see page 21) or regular sour cream

Chipotle Tabasco Sauce (optional)

Tempeh in Coconut-Lemongrass Sauce

Here chipotles are done up Asian style by pairing them with coconut milk, lemongrass, and ginger. Tempeh is a fermented soy product originating from Indonesia. It can be found in natural food stores and is a great vegetarian source of protein and vitamin B12.

In a large nonstick skillet, heat the oil over medium heat. Add the tempeh and cook, turning with tongs, for 8–10 minutes, until lightly browned on all sides. Using a slotted spoon, remove the tempeh to paper towels or a plate and set aside.

Add the onion and pepper to the oil in the skillet, adding a little more oil if necessary, and sauté for about 5 minutes, until softened. Add the ginger and cook for about 2 minutes, until softened, then add the chipotle paste and cook for 2 minutes. Add the lemongrass, coconut milk, maple syrup, and salt to taste. Bring to a simmer, then reduce the heat, cover, and simmer for 10 minutes, stirring occasionally.

Remove the cover, add the tempeh, and cook, uncovered, for 10 minutes, stirring occasionally. Stir in the lime juice. Taste and add additional salt or lime juice if needed. Stir in the cilantro and serve with rice.

SERVES 4

¼ cup extra virgin olive oil, plus extra if needed

8 oz/227 g package tempeh, cut into ½ inch/1 cm squares

1 medium yellow onion, chopped

1 red bell pepper, cored, seeded, and chopped

2-inch/5-cm piece ginger, minced

2 tbsp Chipotle Paste (see page 18) or minced canned chipotle chiles in adobo sauce, or to taste

2 lemongrass stalks, bottom white parts only, cut into thirds

14 fl oz/400 g canned coconut milk

2 tsp maple syrup

1 tbsp fresh lime juice, or to taste

½ cup chopped fresh cilantro

salt

rice, to serve

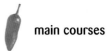

Hot, Sweet & Sour Shrimp

This is a smoky take on the Chinese-American favorite. The heat comes from chipotles—of course—and the tanginess comes from vinegar and tamarind, a sour fruit commonly used in Asian and Latin American cooking. You'll find tamarind paste in Asian and Latin American markets.

To make the marinade, combine the soy sauce, orange juice, sherry, vinegar, tamarind paste, sugar, chipotle paste, and ginger in a small bowl, and whisk to combine and dissolve the sugar. Place the shrimp in a large bowl and toss with 1 tablespoon of the soy sauce mixture. Set aside the shrimp to marinate for 15 minutes.

Heat a wok or large skillet over medium–high heat and add the oil. Add the shrimp and stir-fry for about 2 minutes, until just cooked through. Using a slotted spoon, remove the shrimp to a bowl.

Add more oil to the wok if needed and add the carrots and celery. Cook, stirring for about 2 minutes, until slightly softened. Add the onion and pepper and cook, stirring, for another 2 minutes, or until the vegetables are crisp-tender.

Whisk the reserved marinade. Add the shrimp back to the wok, along with the marinade. Cook, stirring, until cooked through and bubbly, about 2 minutes. Serve with white rice and top with the chopped peanuts.

SERVES 4

2 tbsp soy sauce

¼ cup orange juice

1 tbsp sherry

1 tbsp rice vinegar

1 tsp tamarind paste

2 tbsp packed light brown sugar

2 tbsp Chipotle Paste (see page 18) or minced canned chipotle chiles in adobo sauce, or to taste

½ tsp ground ginger

1 lb/450 g large shrimp, peeled and deveined

1 tbsp peanut oil, plus more if needed

2 medium carrots, cut into thin diagonal strips

2 celery stalks, cut into thin diagonal strips

1 medium yellow onion, cut into thin diagonal strips

1 red bell pepper, cored, seeded, and cut into thin strips

¼ cup chopped peanuts, for garnish

white rice, to serve

Fish Tacos

Assembling the tacos is half the fun in this recipe—use any or all of the toppings suggested, or come up with some of your own.

Chop the fish into pieces and place in a medium bowl. Add the chili powder and season with salt. Stir well to coat the fish with the seasoning.

In a medium skillet, heat the oil over medium–high heat. Add the fish and cook, stirring for about 2 minutes, until cooked through. Add the lime juice and stir until evaporated.

Heat the tortillas by placing them directly over a medium gas flame or in a preheated skillet over medium heat, turning often and watching that they don't burn, for about 20 seconds, until hot.

Place 2 tortillas on each serving plate and top with the fish. Invite your diners to assemble their own tacos, choosing from the suggested toppings. Serve with white rice and refried beans.

SERVES 4

8 oz/225 g skinless red snapper
   fillet
2 tsp Smoky Chili Powder
   (see page 17)
1 tbsp extra virgin olive oil
2 tsp fresh lime juice, or to taste
8 corn tortillas
salt
white rice and refried beans,
   to serve

suggested toppings

Tomatillo Guacamole (see page 32)
Fresh Tomato salsa (see page 9) or
   Green Salsa (see page 10)
Chipotle Tabasco Sauce
grated Monterrey Jack cheese
shredded lettuce

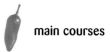

Chicken Adobo

Adobo—meat stewed in a vinegary sauce—is the national dish of the Philippines. Its variations are endless, and here the adobo is enriched with coconut milk and flavored with chipotles.

In a large bowl, combine the coconut milk, vinegar, soy sauce, tamarind paste, sugar, chipotles, garlic, and ginger. Whisk to thoroughly combine.

Place the chicken in a heavy-duty, zip-top bag and pour in the marinade. Seal the bag and refrigerate overnight, turning the chicken a couple of times to evenly marinate.

Place the chicken and marinade in a large saucepan. Bring to a simmer over medium–high heat, then reduce the heat and simmer for 20 minutes, or until the chicken is cooked through. Remove the chicken from the pan and raise the heat. Add the tomatoes and cook for about 20 minutes, until the sauce has reduced by about half. Return the chicken to the pan and heat to warm through. Place in serving dishes and serve over rice.

SERVES 4

14 fl oz/400 g canned coconut milk

1 cup cider vinegar

3 tbsp soy sauce

2 tsp tamarind paste

2 tbsp dark brown sugar

2 tbsp minced canned chipotle chiles
  in adobo sauce

6 garlic cloves, slivered

1 tbsp grated fresh ginger

3½ lb/1.6 kg chicken, cut into serving
  pieces

2 plum tomatoes, quartered

white rice, to serve

South Indian Chicken Curry

While ground cashews add richness to this flavorful home-style curry, chipotles give it a decidedly smoky twist and make for a wonderful combination.

In a food processor, grind the cashews into a fine powder. Leave in the food processor and set aside.

In a medium saucepan, heat 2 tablespoons of the oil over medium–high heat. Add the onion and cook, stirring frequently, for about 10 minutes, until it begins to caramelize. Add the chipotle paste and cook, stirring, for 2 minutes. Add the garam masala, turmeric, and cumin, along with 1 teaspoon of the oil and cook, stirring, for 2 minutes to fry the spices. Add the tomato, reduce the heat to medium, and cook for about 5 minutes, until softened. Add the garlic and ginger and cook for 2 minutes, or until softened.

Remove the spice mixture from the heat and transfer to the food processor with the ground cashews. Add 1¹/₂ cups water and the milk and process until pureed. Return the mixture to the pan and set aside.

In a large nonstick skillet, heat the remaining 3 tablespoons of oil over medium–high heat. Add the cardamom pods, cinnamon, and bay leaves and cook, stirring, for about 2 minutes, until aromatic. Add the chicken pieces and cook, stirring, until just starting to color, about 3 minutes.

Turn the heat for the sauce to medium–high and bring to a simmer. Add the chicken and spices, season with salt to taste, and bring back to a simmer. Reduce the heat, partially cover the pan, and simmer for about 10 minutes, until the chicken is cooked through. Remove the bay leaves and stir in the cilantro. Serve with white rice and naan.

SERVES 4

¼ cup raw cashews
5 tbsp plus 1 tsp vegetable oil
1 medium red onion, chopped
2 tbsp Chipotle Paste (see page 18) or minced canned chipotle chiles in adobo sauce, or to taste
½ tsp garam masala
¼ tsp ground turmeric
¼ tsp ground cumin
1 medium tomato, chopped
3 garlic cloves, minced
1 tbsp minced fresh ginger
2 tbsp milk
3 cardamom pods
½ cinnamon stick, broken into pieces
2 bay leaves
1 whole boneless, skinless chicken breast, about 1 lb/450 g, cut into 1 inch/2.5 cm pieces
1 cup chopped fresh cilantro
salt
white rice and naan bread, to serve

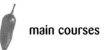

Smoky Hamburgers

Your classic hamburger enhanced with chipotles. Serve with any number of chipotle-spiked toppings.

Work the chili powder and salt into the ground meat with a fork or your clean hands and form into 4 patties.

Preheat a large skillet (preferably cast iron) over medium–high heat until hot. Cook, flipping once, until done to your liking: about 3 minutes per side for rare, 4 minutes per side for medium, and 5 minutes per side for well done.

Place between buns with your choice of toppings.

SERVES 4

2 tbsp Smoky Chili Powder
 (see page 17), or to taste
1 lb 4 oz/550 g ground chuck
salt
4 hamburger buns, split

suggested toppings

Chipotle Ketchup (see page 25)
 or plain ketchup
Chipotle Mustard (see page 25)
 or plain mustard
Quick Pickled Onions (see page 26)
sliced tomatoes
lettuce

Almond-Crusted Steak with Chipotle Butter

If you're in a hurry, you can make this recipe without the almonds—Chipotle Butter on its own adds a beautiful touch to a steak dinner.

Pat the steaks dry and sprinkle with salt. Place the almonds on a plate and press the steaks into the almonds to coat. Set aside for 15 minutes.

In a large heavy skillet, heat the oil over medium–high heat until hot but not smoking. Cook the steaks, one at a time if necessary, about 4 minutes per side for medium–rare. Transfer to a cutting board and let rest 5 minutes before serving.

Slice the steaks, arrange the slices on serving plates, and top with a dollop of chipotle butter. Serve with greens and roasted potatoes.

SERVES 4–6

two 1-inch/2.5-cm thick boneless
   top loin (strip) steaks
1 cup blanched almonds, ground
   to a powder
salt
2 teaspoons vegetable oil
Chipotle Butter (see page 22),
   to serve
greens and roasted potatoes,
   to serve

Chili-Flavored Pork Ribs

Keeping extra rub on hand will make this dish a cinch. You can also use the rub on pork chops, steak, or any grilled meat dish.

To make the smoky rub, combine the chili powder, smoked paprika, mild paprika, oregano, onion powder, and salt in a small bowl. Rub the mixture all over the ribs and set aside for 15 minutes to marinate.

Preheat the oven to 325°F/160°C and line a roasting pan with aluminum foil. Put a rack on the roasting pan. Place the ribs on the rack and roast for 1 – 1 1/2 hours, or until an instant-read thermometer registers 160°F/75°C. Remove from the oven, cut into serving pieces, and serve with mashed potatoes and greens.

SERVES 4

smoky rub

2 tbsp Smoky Chili Powder
   (see page 17)

2 tsp smoked paprika

2 tsp mild paprika

4 tsp dried oregano

2 tsp onion powder

2 tsp salt

4–5 lb/1.8 –2.25 kg country-style
   pork ribs

mashed potatoes, to serve

collard greens or other greens,
   to serve

Pork Loin Chops with Chipotle Mustard Sauce & Spicy Applesauce

This very American dish takes on new heights with the addition of the smoky chipotle.

To make the applesauce, combine all the ingredients in a medium saucepan. Place over medium heat and bring to a simmer. Cover the pan, reduce the heat, and simmer for about 10 minutes, until the apples have softened and are beginning to break down. Coarsely mash the apples with a fork. Set aside while you make the pork, reheating just before serving.

For the pork loin chops, pat the pork dry with paper towels and season with salt. In a large skillet, heat the oil over medium–high heat. Add the pork and cook until just cooked through, 3–5 minutes on each side. Transfer to a plate and tent with foil to keep warm.

Reduce the heat to medium and add the onion to the fat in the pan, adding more oil if needed. Sauté for about 5 minutes, until softened. Add the garlic and sauté for 1 minute. Add the wine and sherry, raise the heat, and cook, stirring to break up any browned bits from the bottom on the pan, for about 5 minutes, until reduced by half. Add the mustard, chili powder, and stock and cook for about 2 minutes, until beginning to thicken. Add the crème fraîche and stir to heat through. Add the spinach and cook, stirring, until wilted, about 2 minutes. Season with salt to taste.

Spoon some rice or noodles onto serving plates. Place the chops on top and finish with the sauce and spinach. Top with a dollop of crème fraîche and serve with the applesauce.

SERVES 4

applesauce
4 McIntosh apples, peeled, cored, and chopped
¾ tsp Smoky Chili Powder (see page 17), or to taste
½ tsp ground cinnamon
2 tsp sherry
pinch of salt
2 tbsp water

pork loin chops
four ½-inch/1-cm thick boneless pork loin chops
1 tbsp extra virgin olive oil, plus extra if needed
½ medium onion, finely chopped
1 garlic clove, finely chopped
¼ cup dry white wine
2 tbsp sherry
2 tsp Chipotle Mustard (see page 25)
1 tsp Smoky Chili Powder (see page 17), or to taste
1¼ cups chicken stock
2 tbsp crème fraîche, plus extra to serve
2 cups fresh spinach leaves
salt
white rice or egg noodles, to serve